"Believe Me"

Trump Poems

VOLUME ONE

by Claude Mayers

An **OCEAN POETRY** Publication • Gainesville, Georgia

CLAUDE MAYERS

"Believe Me" - Trump Poems Volume One

Copyright © 2018 Claude Mayers
All rights reserved.
This book created in the United States of America.

Any properly footnoted quotation of up to 10 sequential words may be used without permission, as long as the total number of words does not exceed 20 words. For longer quotations or for a greater number of total words quoted, written permission from the publisher is required.

This book is available through Amazon and worldwide via multiple platforms.

For further information you may email
    claudemayersny@yahoo.com

Cover Graphic Design:
Lutha Leahy-Miller/Claude Mayers/Farrell Rene Miller

Cover Photo Inset: Gage Skidmore (see Attributions page)

Interior Layout: Claude Mayers

ISBN: 978-0-9753832-1-6

Publisher: Ocean Poetry, P.O. Box 186, Murrayville, Ga 30564

This book of poems is dedicated to the United States of America and its various glorious mix of people of all backgrounds and ethnicities.

"Hot diggity dog, ziggity boom, what you DO to me. . ."

  -- from 1956 #1 tune written by Al Hoffman and Dick Manning. Recorded by Perry Como and the Ray Charles Singers.

Claude Mayers joins the fearless ranks of Yevtushenko, Neruda, Pasolini, among others, daring to bear Poetry into the realm of Politics.
- Canio Pavone, Founder of the Hamptons, New York's Most Historic Bookstore 'Canio's' (actually located in Sag Harbor).

These poems document life in the madhouse that has gripped the world since that fateful November hijacking of civilization as we knew it. Buckle your seatbelts, it's quite a ride!
- Avram Chetron, Activist, Musician, Teacher, Engineer; Ashland, Oregon

Mayers' poems ring true in ways that discomfort us, which we must come to understand in order to take appropriate action. Here's hoping that his words assist in unlocking the divisions and fears which have gripped our country over these past 2 years.
- Dr. Andrew Harris, Psychologist, Worldwide Adventurer, Photographer

Mayers' poetry, filled with passion and anger, will resonate with those who are in despair for the state of our nation brought upon by the current disgraceful – and possibly treasonous – president and his administration.
- Jerry Nussbaum PhD, Sociology Professor [Rtd.], SF Bay Real Estate Broker

Introduction

It has been over a year now since Donald Trump surprised the world with his iconoclastic* ascent to become the most powerful man in the world: President of the United States of America. His style of action pleases his 'base' and horrifies the other half of a country that had been the leader of the Free World. Now priorities are being re-organized, often with dysfunction and intrigue. These poems that follow track the journey of the controversial figure who willed himself into office, amidst a political atmosphere that we have never seen before, in a most dramatic dangerous time . . .

*characterized by attack on cherished beliefs or institutions

Table of Contents

Believe Me	4
New Year's Day 2017	5
American People	7
38 Trademarks	9
Press Conference	10
Donald Admits To No Mistakes	11
He Knows What Is Right, He's The President	13
I Will Let My Saber Rattle	16
Invincible	17
Play Dominoes	19
Wilbur Ross	23
Amass Considerable Portable Holes	26
Foreigners Suing For Mining Rights In Missouri	28
Lauding President Andrew Jackson (Trump Is)	30
Donald Babbling About War Recklessly	32
Bot Attack On America	34
Where Is The Outrage At Russia!!??	38
Putin Reaps The Booty	40
Silently Stealing Our Privacy	43
Devin Nunes	46
Bugging Out	48
Purge State Attorneys Haiku	51

Preet Bharara	52
Integrity On A Bender	55
Now We Know (Comey's Firing)	57
When I Did What I Did And Why I Did It	60
Pathological Liar	62
Chaos And The Cool Calm Complete	65
Trump Administration Forbids Use Of 7 Taboo Words (*Italicized*) By Center For Disease Control (CDC) Scientists	68
Trump Declares Jerusalem The Capital Of Israel	71
First Commutation (Of A Money Launderer)	75
Morning Meeting With Chuck And Nancy	78
Envision Misogyny	80
For Roy Moore	83
Jeff Sessions – USA Attorney General – April 23, 2017	88
Trump And Nixon	92
Wait A Few Weeks Before You're Impeached	94
Exiled To Siberia	97
Black NFL Player	102
N-Word on LeBron's Gate	106
Why Ignore Russian Cyber-Infiltration Of Our Nation (USA)?	109

CLAUDE MAYERS

"BELIEVE ME" - TRUMP POEMS

January 3, 2018 – one day before publication
           of <u>Fire And Fury</u> by Michael Wolff

"There's clearly no conversations taking place in this White House about what's happening in Iran, the situation in North Korea, the provocations the President made toward Pakistan publicly… not that the substance of his criticisms is wrong, but should be delivered privately.

The world is boiling here at the beginning of two thousand and eighteen [2018]. And the whole country is trapped in this dystopian-dysfunctional-reality-show metastasized-into-a-horror-movie/soap-opera that plays out every day on the TV. It's quite extraordinary. But it's also quite dangerous. The qualities of character that we're seeing, the recklessness, the incompetence, the malfeasance, the self-interest, in the most powerful office in the world, present great danger to this country, and, frankly, to free peoples everywhere."

   - Steve Schmidt on Lawrence O'Donnell Show Jan 3, 2018
31-32 minutes into show

Belie: two letters shorter than the word *'believe'*

To represent falsely; misrepresent; contradict;

        as to *belie* the facts

Believe: To have faith or confidence in the strength, truth, or integrity of any one or anything; trust [as in: 'Trust Me' or 'Believe Me']

Page 183 Funk And Wagnall's Dictionary,
        published 1900
          [edited]

"BELIEVE ME" - TRUMP POEMS

Donald Trump

- often says 'Believe Me' during speeches,
- usually added after speaking the truth or a lie,
- has lied or made misleading statements more than 2000 times since becoming President, as per Washington Post January 10, 2018

https://www.washingtonpost.com/news/fact-checker/wp/2018/01/10/president-trump-has-made-more-than-2000-false-or-misleading-claims-over-355-days/?utm_term=.a19abfa96058

Believe Me

Believe me

I know what gets you

Angry and inflamed

I play the game

I ride your backs

I compliment your hate

The lies I tell

Forgotten in your faith

                                       in me

New Year's Day Poem 2017

Actually
There is no reason
To sustain the belief
That somehow we should expect
Relief from our problems
The new administration
Will only certainly worsen the situation
With the greed and grief
They will inflict
On our broken backs
And weepy wishes

There was promise in the streets
        progress building
        openness gilding the future's skies
        that now will brown
        with fossil fuel dealers
        drilling in restricted wilderness
        that shall be served
        to the gluttonous elites
        for profit and deceit

There may be repression

Racism gone ballistic
Hate festering
Narcissism nesting
In our paranoid thinking
That the police
Will kill our people
With their military weapons
And tanks attacking rebellious young idealists

You can walk to the steeple
Listening to the Sunday bells ringing
So peacefully
Ready to worship spiritually
But whose god
Approves such diabolic perversion
Of our sacred democracy

We took justice for granted
Not expecting strident evil
Dwells in the manic officials
We stupidly elected
To strip our country
Of its essential needs

American People

People are unconcerned
About truths and details
Ridiculed by the eminent
The irate
The perturbed
They are struggling
To provide essential moneys
That will fund a lifestyle
Excruciatingly deteriorating
Causing them to work more hours
Than ever
Though the future was so promising
So modern
So advanced
People wanting the benefits
But not the intrusion
Taxing their patience
Demanding their attention
Which they'd prefer to give
To basic needs
That build prosperous happiness
Which retracts behind a mist
Becoming daily more distant
While the rich sit back
Collecting more returns
On their investments
Congress catering to please them
Enrich themselves

Ignoring blatant attacks
On our sovereignty
Too many desperate individuals
Pushed to blame the other
For their own descent
Into the economy's nadir
Crisis suppressed across their consciousnesses
Mysfocused on fear and hate
As treasonous criminals' deeds
Continue to be revealed
People just wanting
Assistance in their misery
Not responsibility as citizens
To understand the picture
Blurred by the vindictive
Further irritating their feelings
Feeding voluntary ignorance
Of what seems too confusing
For their innocence
About politics and malfeasance

Spring Chang: Beijing-based attorney representing Donald Trump

Emoluments clause – from Article 1 of USA Constitution – prohibits public officials from accepting any present or Emolument from any foreign state without the Consent of the Congress.

38 Trademarks

Spring Chang
Says it's not unusual
38 trademarks sailing through
The approval process
In Beijing
For Donald Trump
And his corporate interests
Raising the question
Of defiance of the emoluments clause
By our acquisitive president
Still not releasing his tax returns
Nor divesting himself of his businesses
Loving to complete a big deal
For the benefit of himself
But what about his responsibility
His integrity
As Commander-In-Chief of our country?

written January 12, 2017, 8 days before Trump's Inauguration 1-20-17

Press Conference

When the audience is hostile
And you're taking amoxil
How can you be at peace
Or relaxed
Being jounced by these
Irritating hacks
Rudely asking questions
Shouting out
Calling "Mister President"
Making you anxious
A whole room of people
Contentious
Pretentious
Not your fawning followers
Cheering your rants
Attacking protestors
As you extend your grasp
Of bullying tactics

Donald Admits To No Mistakes

I will not admit

To making any mistakes

I have a seventh sense

That made me so successful

I'm a great judge

Of what works

And what a loser chooses

As his mediocre option

I alert to only the best

The highest forms

The unique attributes

From which profit can be squeezed

Others cannot perceive

What I brand

For the future

Heed my detonating warning

There's danger looming

Listen to my words

Then forget what I say

He Knows What Is Right, He's The President (Trump)

Everything he does is great

Even if he lies every day

We forget what he said

        what he tweeted

The past a swamp we're draining

As he leads the way

Round the regulators

Over those transgender agents

Serving in our military

Their hormones supplied

At our Obama expense

Electroshock therapy will cure

Their abominated brains

Justice is not negotiable

He knows what is right

He's the President

Who tweets what he feels

Without hampering reflection

Or Isis immigrants

Granted anything

But the DEATH PENALTY!

We love how he

Calls out those black football players

Taking a knee out of disrespect

For the anthem and flag

We have to preserve the white race

From the darkening hordes

Trying to enter our space

Taking our jobs

Ruining our country

Russia a ruse

Not an enemy now

No they're an ally

Papadopoulos a coffee boy

He hardly remembers

His memory so perfect

His money laundering suspended

His divesting no issue

Because he's such a successful businessman

Who knows how to fix our economy

There's plenty more oil

And land for the rich to take

As the wealth slowly

Will trickle down

Blessing our God-given nation

I Will Let My Saber Rattle
(For Donald Trump #62)

I will
Fight the battle
I will let
My saber rattle
Am I afraid
Of looking stupid
Nefarious
Bold
Or wisely inscrutable
Patriotic
Despotic
How would you know
My devastation of the neutral
Is only a blow
That history will enamor
With gobs of admiration
As I let my saber rattle

Invincible

You seem to believe
That nothing will deter you
No obstacles will appear
Blocking your oblivious faith
In how you will fare
Against all enemies

You are brave and strong
There no superior forces
That might possibly linger in ambush
Above you
You always seeing clearly
Powerful and
        Fierce
Your body hard
Your virtue perfect

There no way
You will meet defeat
Without breaking its back
Or stewing its meat

Omniscient and true
Others may struggle
But never you

**Sunshine reflecting off the facets
Of your vibrant fortune
You will forever succeed
Unimpeded by doubt
Until the sky freezes over
A cracked arctic blue**

schnook: An incompetent person who is deserving of pity but also likeable;
a customer easily persuaded, a sucker (H.L. Mencken, American language);
a gullible simpleton more to be pitied than despised (Yiddish);
a person easily taken advantage of; a person easily imposed upon or cheated;
a dupe or dope; a fool; origin (Oxford Living Dictionaries) 1940s: perhaps from
German Schnucke – small sheep.

Play Dominoes

You can go there

Play dominoes

With those who believe

They are being cheated

By the liberal elite

With their soft pinkish feet

In fluffy sheep slippers

Expanding on sharing the country

With those who don't believe

Our propagandized story

The white race starting to shrink

Into the rainbow coalition

Growing naturally

As the light shines

On civil tourists

Aghast at what is happening

Racial supremacy headlining

CLAUDE MAYERS

One Afternoon

In Domino Park

The terribly overrated

Value of equality

Methedrine speeding up the cracking texture

Of love

      Behooving tolerance

The rich biting off more wealth

Than their hearts can hold

The banks clamping their greedy lawyers

Upon the shnooks

Who hate environmental laws

While their homes are lost

To the foreclosure lords

Wilbur Ross
Secretary of Commerce
Former majority owner and Vice-Chairman of
Board of Directors of Bank of Cyprus, notorious
money-laundering bank for Russians*
(Ross' fellow co-chair appointed by
Vladimir Putin**).

*http://www.businessinsider.com/trump-russia-connection-and-wilbur-ross-2017-5

**http://www.nationalmemo.com/wilbur-ross-next-trump-official-targeted-mueller-probe/

Wilbur Ross

Little old white man

With Ben Franklin frameless spectacles

Will now head Trump's Commerce Department

As Secretary

After organizing foreclosures

Of countless citizens' homes

Being banned from pension fund overseeing

Of workers

Like those who died at West Virginia's

Sago Mine

Where he knew about

Various previous roof collapses

And toxic gasses entrapped

Threatening miners' lives

Before the historic fatal collapse

Finally occurred

Reached the television screens

Of millions of Americans

Ross engineering breathtaking contracts

Eliminating unions

        health care

        pensions for miners

While he paid one hundred million dollars

For a Rene Magritte painting

Owns actually forty three Magrittes himself

Art the great investment

For billionaires like him

The leader

The Grand Swipe

Of secret Wall Street Society

Kappa Beta Phi

Since 2012

Where losers are lampooned

And bigwigs banter

And roast each other

Partying and drinking

Singing altered lyrics

To well-known show tunes

Ross a graduate of Yale University

And Harvard Business School

Now about to oversee the USA economy

Lacking compassion

Bathing in fortune

Amongst a cabinet of wealthsters

Some saying

They will divest from investments

To give the country

           something back

Padding their egos

Accomplishing more cut-throat success

In Trump's aggressive quest for Greatness

Amass Considerable Portable Holes

Amass considerable portable holes
So no one will know
Where the story goes
Powerful vacuums suck up
The energy of scoundrels and sibyls
        monsters and miracles
There will be no vengeance
Because nothing is visible
The space deeply black
Full of silence

The party hack
Ruminates on the back
Of misled citizens
The truth is groomed
Then launched to the moon
Where it will orbit
Until infinity ends

There will be turns at the bend

Immoderate suspense

The holes transported

In convoys of camouflaged vans

Exuding false mist

Odors inducing amnesia

Deception adrift

The future listing on a ship

In a typhoon ocean

The past rasping on a dash

Of crashed dumpster ovens

Leaking blue gravy

While chefs praise

Humble apprentices

Trying to fill

Their baking bowls

With pastry dough

And gourmet soul

      abundantly overflowing

Foreigners Suing For Mineral Rights In Missouri

Foreigners suing for mineral rights in Missouri

Abolish the Environmental Protection Agency (EPA)

Brainwashed Americans vouch for the

Rich being successful

Thus they know what to do

When the environment is screwed

The plants and the animals

The air and the water

Having no voice to protest

The treatment they receive

At the blatant hands

Of opportunists and profiteers

Hardly caring for foolish citizens

Wanting to put their faith somewhere

Preferably in a strongman / bully

Who lies spontaneously

Has no remorse

For how his untruths affect the future

And the people and plants and animals

Adversely polluted by greed

Unethical execution of orders

Signed in flashing paparazzi light

The President smiling brutally

Foreigners and business barons

Not having to clean up the mess they make

Once they rob the Earth

Covered acutely by effusive propaganda

The environment surrounding life forms

Choking futilely

Without respect

Or comprehending duty

Lauding President Andrew Jackson (Trump Is…)

You were angry about the civil war

With your slaves

And your treatment of Native Americans

The Trail of Tears after your Indian Removal Act

Killed thousands of forced evacuees

Marching at the end of bayonets

From Georgia and Alabama

                    across the Mississippi River

While whites stole their land

Our seventh President

Lauded by our 45th

Who admires strongmen and dictators

Though ill-informed about historic details

Complimenting Kim Jong-un as a "smart cookie"

Duterte of the Philippines who wants to

Kill 100,000 criminals without trials

(Has killed 8 thousand so far via

 Roving death squads)

Trump commending his *popularity*

Also admiring dictator Vladimir Putin

Hanging a portrait of Andrew Jackson

In the Oval Office of the White House

Claiming Jackson said

"There's No Reason For This"

In reference to our civil war

Which began in 1861

While Jackson died in 1845

Re Duterte of Philippines:

http://news.nationalpost.com/news/world/duterte-gave-infamous-philippines-dictator-a-heros-burial-while-the-vice-president-called-him-a-murderer

Donald, Babbling About War Recklessly . . .

You could go on

Babbling about war recklessly

Filling up your self-congratulatory tank

Of ego

Inflamed by power

The nuclear codes dancing in your head

While we live in dread

Fearing your psychotic behavior

Your fawning sycophants

Kneeling at your feet

Wheeling in truckloads of praise

Shafting the people

Who see through your insanity

But are unable

To impeach you immediately

Before you destroy the threatened planet

Upon which we all have to exist

In harmony

        and peace

Valery Gerasimov: Russian General, Chief of Russian Armed Forces, currently plotting with Vladimir Putin to wage cyberwarfare at a 4 to 1 ratio to physical warfare.*

Bot Attacks: the word 'Botnet' combines the words 'robot' and 'network.' Cyberhackers use special Trojan viruses to breach the security of attacked computers, take control of these, and organize all the infected machines into a network of 'bots' that the hackers can remotely manage to i.e., send out the same message to millions of computers and their unsuspecting users.
Troll: internet slang for person or entity on internet who/which sows discord by starting quarrels or upsetting people, by posting inflammatiory, extraneous, or off-topic messages in an online community.**

Bot Attack On America

Back to the beat

Back to the retreat

To concentrate

On the meat

Of what's being tweeted

Automatically

By cybergeniuses

Waging infowarfare

General Valery Gerasimov -- on right with headphones -- Chief of Russian Armed Forces. Currently plotting with Vladimir Putin to wage cyberwarfare at a 4:1 ratio to physical warfare. States that today most wars are not declared

Through social media

Bots send out cloned messages

Of hate or porn or thoughts unseemly

To defeat our freedom

To communicate intelligently

With other people

Affecting elections

And reputations

Russians arrange trolling operations

To select the objects of their missions

For power and control

Of the opposition

Putin and Gerasimov*

Strategizing how to win

The battle of public opinion

For their country

    their profit

While American ideologues

Plod through the muck they generate

Missing the widespread deployment

Of damaging bots

Attacking the enemies of Russia

From perhaps tiny Albania

        or even Macedonia

** https://usa.kaspersky.com/resource-center/threats/botnet-attacks
Internet bot

https://en.wikipedia.org/wiki/Internet_bot

Where Is The Outrage At Russia!!??

Where is the outrage

At Russia

Hacking our elections

Are you complicit

    illicit

    can't say a word

    perturbed

    disturbed

Why not yell loudly

And immoderately

Denouncing Putin's cyberwarriors

Oh collusionists may be

Hidden in your underworld

The mob

The oligarchs

How to absolve the innocent

How you evade

Any passionate harangue

Against foreign criminals

Possibly operating

With individuals

Active in your campaign

Lending you money

Suborning your unwitting

Or witting

To treasonously enact

What Putin wants

While you joke with spying diplomats

Worming out your vanity

So you spout nut job revelations

That degrade

Your own nation

Putin Reaps The Booty

Putin bans his main opponent
From the upcoming election
That will give him six more years to rule
A nation where protests are harshly prohibited
A totalitarian nation
That has not severed Siberia
From its flanks yet
Political prisoners still being tortured or killed

And now
Vladimir has a patsy to play
To vault Mother Russia
Above the wastes of western democratic ruin
Cyberwar successful
As polarized Americans
Fail to halt the glut of greed
From suffocating the truth
That they patriotically rebuke
Botting and false memes
Herding the cows off the cliff
While Vladimir continues to lie
About his participation

Vladimir Putin

In the attack
On sacred institutions
Trump echoing the brute
As if he too
Was powerful and smart
Crippling his country
While Putin wins another battle
Running up the score
Against fools
Who pose and posture
For admiring suitors
Pumping up the praise
Expecting inordinate gains
For whatever corruption they sow
While Vladimir reaps the booty

Silently Stealing Our Privacy
(In The Midst Of The News Whirlwind....)

In the midst of the news whirlwind
The House Intelligence Committee chairman
Changing vehicles in the night
To avoid detection of him going to the White House
Paul Manafort ex-Trump campaign manager
        spending his laundered Russian millions
On New York real estate
Paying cash for exorbitantly priced apartments
One in Trump Tower
Using shell companies for the purchases
Then transferring ownership to himself
For zero dollars
Then garnering huge loan monies
Via mortgaging the lienless properties
The mind spinning
At such rapacious audacity
Wondering about treason
A message runs across the bottom of the screen
That Congress has passed a bill
Silently stealing our privacy

Allowing internet companies
To sell our browsing history
And our location data
So we can be tracked like lemmings
Via satellite and greed
    fear and government intrusion
By corrupted politicians
Claiming they want to shrink or abolish
The government they deploy
To take away freedom
In the name of anti-terrorism
Pimping for the corporations
And the fools twisted by power
Ravaging their souls
As they follow us
Wherever we go
Or surf the information highway
Soon to be shackled by spycatchers
And phantom tollbooth operatives
Peppering us with pop-ups
Inadvertently revealing to us
Where we parked our car

"BELIEVE ME" - TRUMP POEMS

Devin Nunes (R-California)
(Adam Schiff behind him (D-California))

Nunes is Once-Recused Chairman of the
House Intelligence Committee
Labelled 'Trump's Stooge'
by the Sacremento Bee 1-24-18*

*http://www.sacbee.com/opinion/editorials/article196449149.html

Devin Nunes: Conservative Representative from California; once-recused Chairman of House Intelligence Committee; famous for car-switching secretive middle-of-the-night-episode to visit White House to fetch already utilized documents to protect Donald Trump's role in Russia interference investigation. Wikipedia quotes him stating that members of environmental lobby were 'followers of neo-Marxist, socialist, Maoist or Communist ideals.'

Devin Nunes

There's nothing there

To investigate

Our party denies

Imperceptible contusions

Of the spirit of the law

God carries us

Over many bridges

Beyond the devil's hands

We know when wrong

Has been committed

But those multiple conversations

With the Russians

During campaign days

Why should we think

Any collusion transpired

Though the press conspires

To spread their lies

How the impossible can undermine

Our practical negation

Of circumstantial observations

There no proof evident

Shouting from the wall

Or the woofing bass speakers

Out of control

We try to moderate

The panic alerted

By the liberals

In their bitter groves

Saying there was hacking of computers

By cyberspacial looters

At workstations planted

Round the globe

Co-ordinated by Putin

Who our President loves

As Isis Muslims rebuke us

And our concerns with safety

For our precious patriotic national soul

Bugging Out

I can't sleep
I feel the bugs
Infiltrating my skin
Listening in
To all my conversations
With the Prussians and the Russians
The moguls and the winners
Who make this country great
Obama a hateful sinner
Wiretapping my New York office
I KNOW he did it
He's the one responsible
I have to tweet this out
Without any proof
It's 6 A.M.
Not the time to ask my staff
Or the Intel community

I'm certain I am right
My followers love me
Regardless of my fidelity
To the truth
Or alternative facts
Or fake news
I tweet from the heart
I act by how I feel
That's why my cheering fans
Wait for my words
About those leaks
By these traitors
Who're trying to do me in

That Clapper saying the FBI
Never authorized any wiretapping
He the National Intelligence director
During the campaign
That swept me into the Presidency
No one thought that I'd win

Not even Vladimir Putin

I'm angry that anybody doubts me
I've thrown Priebus and Steve Bannon
Off Air Force One
For my trip to Mar-A-Lago this weekend

Maybe I need to take a calming drink
Or perhaps a secret sedative
So I can relax
                fall back to sleep . . .

Purge State Attorneys Haiku

Purge state attorneys

Eliminate opponents

To corruptive deals

Preet Bharara

U.S. Attorney for the southern district

Of New York

Investigating Wall Street

        Trump Tower

        Roger Ailes' sexual harassment cases

While questionable deals are being made

Money laundering claims

No Trump tax returns filed

To aid the evaluation of the narrative

Preet already jailing two prominent

New York State Democratic leaders for corruption

Though nominated by Democrat Barack Obama

Back in 2009

Asked by President Trump and

Attorney General Sessions to stay on

Into their administration back in November 2016

Then suddenly ordered to resign on March 10th 2017

With 45 other state attorneys

Preet refusing

Giving him an additional 24 hours plus

To collect data

Do whatever he thought was correct to do

Before the President officially fired him

On the following day

Now rumor has it

Roger Ailes' attorney

Defending him in Preet's court

Will be nominated to replace Preet

While Ailes is being investigated

For paying off various sexual harassment plaintiffs

With FOX corporation money

Never informing FOX stockholders

The suspicious purchase of the 666 Building

    In Manhattan by the shady Chinese Anbang corporation

    For 2.85 billion dollars

    Making it the most expensive building sale in the history of the USA

    Massively profiting the Kushners

    Jared Kushner Trump's trusted advisor and son-in-law

Transpiring in the southern district

Perhaps also pushing the President

To fire Preet

Before he might start investigating the transaction

Preet leaving his office Saturday

To beloved applause

From New Yorkers appreciative

Of his great work

Integrity on display

Under a cloud of nefarious treachery

Integrity On A Bender

I have been thwarted

The deal has been aborted

Devious behavior

Integrity on a bender

Drunk in the street again

Lost its head

As it rolls

      down the hill

           to the beach

Where it will make a muted splash

Then slowly

      float

           away . . . .

James Comey – FBI Director

until fired by Donald Trump 5-9-17
for investigating Russia's intrusion
into USA elections, possible collusion

Now We Know
(Comey's Firing)

Now we know
The lies were told
In flagrant disregard
Of democracy
    the constitution
Bullying the FBI director
To stop the investigation
Of the Russian hacking
Of our elections
Specifically Mike Flynn
Comey writing down his memos
To notate what happened
His practice
When required
By various situations
Trump saying it was Hillary's emails
It was Rod Rosenstein
Who came to him
Recommending the firing of Comey

No it was him
The President himself
Who made the decision
He tired of this Russian hoax
Comey wasn't doing a good job
The White House staff
Pushed over the cliff
Having to explain his words
His erratic behavior
His giving to the two Sergeys
Classified information
As the commander-in-chief
It his privilege to do this
Such information then immediately de-classified
But the spy or spies in the city he named
Now could be outed
                        killed
                        tortured
By Isis operatives
If Russia betrayed him or her
                        the nation that trusted us
                        not to reveal what it had given us

                        unlikely to trust us again
This threatening the security of our country
The two Sergeys
        Russian diplomats
        in the Oval Office
        without any American reporters present
        only fellow Russians
        still laughing
        at Trump's foolish naiveté
        somehow beholden to Putin
        dashing the sanctity of the USA

When I Did What I Did And Why I Did It

When I did
What I did
And why
        I did it
Are not to be explained
Transparently or errantly
Trouble is plaguing me
Citizens enraged at me
Prevent Truth to clearly be serviced
We have to go around the corner
Weave a coat of many colors
Manifest the obvious
Behind a feeble fabric
That shelters
What I promised
From how accomplishment gets done
I have a lot of fun
Wielding weighty challenges
That are not diplomatically sound

Then I backtrack

Exploit the loopholes

In the compact

Pamper legal alibis

That let the lambs think

They are the tigers

That the elephant stomps

Into the bloody ground

I do not have to offer denials

For the imperial wizards of justice

I do not learn from my mistakes

Because I don't make any

Life is full of chaos

Launching points created

From myriad opportunities

That can be embraced

Built upon

Bounding over choppy seas

With the albatrosses and the whales

Never revealing exactly how I feel

Or how next I shall betray the nation

Pathological Liar

The words come out

North and south

Perpetually spouted

From your fountain mouth

A river crowd

A rally mob

Chant your words

Your vaunted pouts

Brains numb

Lips shouting

What you espouse

Coarsely drowning

In livid doubt

Of apparitions

    poor renditions

Shaped about

Your lying rout

Of truth

And enemy opposition

Left demolished

On hills

In valleys

Cartoon by Gary Oliver

Chaos And The Cool Calm Complete

When the chaos
Confuses the cool calm complete
Sitting on their seats
Watching the sunset
In peace
It is time
To get out the sheets
Of preparation
That mobilize both the elite
And the depleted
While the complete attempt
To manage discreetly
How the chaos to meet
And calm
At least on their street
The President orchestrating
What bumbles through his head
Transferring it to the souls of the people
Rabidly eating their meat
          and cheese
While savages accentuate
          their natural existentialism
Surviving between the trees
One with their environment
Not sucking the oil out of sacred grounds
Blasting sonar waves about the sea
The traffic gnarled in civilization's cities
There hateful opposition brewing

As the chaos crescendos toward an apogee
The cool calm complete
Quietly meditating
On the various maddened energies
Letting them go
Letting them be
Until they are exhausted
Compost and debris
Feeding future love
While the jittery President
Gulps his super high-powered tea
Watching TV
Tweeting like a woodpecker
Tapping upon his phone's tiny slimy keys

Photo by Raed Mansour

Trump administration informed CDC (Center For Disease Control) on 12-15-17 that the following 'words' were forbidden to be used: fetus, vulnerable, science-based, evidence-based, transgender, entitlement, diversity.
George Orwell is British author who wrote the classic totalitarian state novel <u>1984</u> from whence comes the still-lingering paranoid thought 'Big Brother is watching you' . . .
Round-Up – world's most widely used herbicide, with glyphosate as its main chemical ingredient, which passes through the placenta, can cause mutations in the fetus, banned in Denmark. Recent studies have found it in air and water; deemed 'probable carcinogen' by World Health Organization (WHO) in March 2015*.

Trump Administration Forbids Use
Of 7 Taboo Words (*Italicized*)
By Center For Disease Control (CDC) Scientists

Do I have any *entitlement* to the future

I'm old

I'm a child

I'm disabled

I'm *transgender*

I'm female

I'm *vulnerable*

I'm Native American

My Medicaid's been stolen (my Medicare's next)

Also my internet

My Planned Parenthood access

My social security threatened

My sacred land violated

By another lying President

I'm opioid dependent

I'm a *fetus* mutated

By poorly tested chemicals

That pass through the placenta

Round-Up on the wheat

   in the water

   tainting the air I must breathe

Glyphosate I repeat

Is spreading everywhere

There so much *diversity*

That we need

That makes our country great

The conclusion is *evidence-based*

    science-based

Our studies widely dissected

Our recommendations openly shared

As George Orwell weeps

In the deceit

Forbidding Truth's speech

From the lips of CDC workers

Our doctors incredulous

Our professors emeritus

Knowing how Big Brother intercedes

First taking our freedom

Piece by piece

Then herding us like sheep

Into brainwash meekdom

Sterilizing our thinking

Unless we stand outraged together

Against the greediest censors

Declaring what words

Incriminate themselves

As they list

        the seven taboo terms

Italicized in this verbiage

* http://www.nature.com/doifinder/10.1038/nature.2015.17181

Trump Declares Jerusalem The Capital Of Israel

What gives you the right

To declare Jerusalem the capital of Israel

Angering Muslims and Christians

Whose city it is also

Your power is too broad

For a man lacking the capacity

To understand the repercussions

Of his actions

Your audacity is outrageous

Thinking by being decisive and emphatic

You can solve the conundrum

Of the Middle East

Where the devotees and disciples of Christ

And Mohammed, the Pope and Moses

Have been embattled

For hundreds of years

Killing each other

Loving their separate versions

Of God and Allah

Jehovah and Adonai

Jewish settlements in what is supposed

To be Arab Palestine

Hate being created

As Israel rules

The land beside the Sinai

With a heavy hand

                        today

Intifada

Land mines along the Lebanese border

The USA has tried to lead the way

To a two-state solution for the region

Aiming for a lasting peace

Respect for each other

Across wisely drawn borders

Israel receives the third most American foreign aid

Of any country on Earth

Followed by Egypt

Then Jordan*

We can influence these nations' politics

Without worsening their horror

Now thanks to you

Fresh firestorms are flaming

In the planet's

Most problematic tinderbox

With your insensitive ego

You have provoked

More desperation

And explosions of frustration

Study your history

Comprehend the tenuous nature of the peace process

That you have stomped

Your bone-spurred feet into

Further destabilizing a region

Requiring brilliant even-handed diplomacy

Not impulsive chaos

Which you specialize

In creating

Smirking like a demented demagogue

*Iraq and Afghanistan are #1 and #2, receiving ~$5 billion each in USA aid in 2016 – from USAID.gov
[Israel receives $3.1 billion; Egypt & Jordan ~$1.2 billion each; total USA foreign aid 2016 = $49 Billion]

'Sholom Rubashkin was sentenced to 27 years in jail for money laundering and a $27 million fraud. He ran the family business – 'Agriprocessors' - in Iowa, which was the country's largest kosher meat-processing company. His prosecution came after federal authorities raided the plant and arrested 389 illegal immigrants in 2008 - people who were subjected to work under atrocious conditions, threatened by the spectre of deportation.' * **

First Commutation* **
(Of A Money Launderer)

Why would the President

Choose a money launderer

As the first person

Whose sentence he commutes

Is it a common empathy

A kosher rabbi's treachery

Akin to his own

Desperate actions

Trying to prevent another bankruptcy

Of his business empire

    his maimed insidious soul

* https://www.yahoo.com/news/trump-commutes-sentence-kosher-meatpacking-executive-225329336--politics.html

** https://www.washingtonpost.com/opinions/why-all-the-sympathy-for-this-slaughterhouse-executive/2017/12/22/3521bbc6-e6a2-11e7-ab50-621fe0588340_story.html?utm_term=.6b2e272d4816

"BELIEVE ME" - TRUMP POEMS

Chuck Schumer   Nancy Pelosi

Democrat   Democrat
Senator   Representative
New York   California

Morning Meeting With Chuck and Nancy

When you will be meeting

With the opposition

Sabotaging your own daft position

Telling lies about the two leaders

You have invited

To pass a budget

Preventing a government shutdown

Tweeting against your best interests

A few hours before their arrival

You don't see a deal!

Saying they want illegal immigrants

Flooding into our country unchecked

Are weak on crime

And want to substantially RAISE taxes

When your tax cut plan for the rich

Which they bluntly bash

Raises taxes in fact

On the middle class

And the poor

Your lies too brash

Your diplomacy too crass

They deciding not to attend

The photo-op you have staged

An empty chair

On either side of you

On the waiting table

Their engraved name plates

Your insulting counterproductive insanity

Requiring an apology

Which you'll never give

As you rashly sink deeper

Into your political grave

Envision Misogyny

Why do I have to envision

A man fondling women's breasts

In an elevator

Without consent

Misogyny

Dignity aggressed

By our leader's dialogue

Attacking people

For their weight or their race

When I want to embrace peace

Feel beauty grace my face

A cool wind cleansing

My active body

Love in my heart

Others not excluding me

Or denigrated citizens

Having their rights usurped

Their hopes splayed

On the pavement

Chaos spreading through an environment

Of mistrust

Gender behavior losing its center

Men unsure if they should

Express their superior physical strength

Without restraint

Suppress women

As bothersome and inferior

Take their gains

Of past decades

Summarily away

As the President rants and raves

Roy Moore

Racist Homophobe
Alabama

Twice removed from post as
Alabama Chief Justice
Defeated in 2017 Senate Election
But 68% White Voters
80% White Evangelicals
52% White Female College Grads
Voted For Him in Alabama

Alabama election exit poll results - Washington Post
https://www.washingtonpost.com/graphics/2017/politics/alabama-exit-polls/

KKK Pettus bridge: refers to the 1965 Selma civil rights march over the bridge named after the Confederate brigadier general, former U.S. Senator from Alabama, and Grand Dragon of the Ku Klux Klan, Edmund Pettus (1821-1907)

For Roy Moore, Defeated Alabama Senate Candidate 2017

America's decent people

Were frightened

By the implications

Of your predicted victory

For the Senate race in Alabama

You effused bigotry hatred homophobia

Unapologetic insensitivity

To voters other than your

Sexist white supporters

Who believed your blatant denials

Of sexual advances

Upon high school girls

When you were the power-wielding bully

District attorney in your early thirties

You invoked God

To exact your hypocritical moral view
Of the world
Romancing back to the times of slavery
Saying that was when America
Was last truly great
You ready to rampage
Through the halls of Congress
Battering the brains of Democracy
Into senselessness
Endorsed by a lunatic President
And donor-driven politicians
Pimping for the rich
Pushing to cut taxes for them
While raising rates for everyone else

You sure of your gun twirling self
On your horse
Hiding behind the Ten Commandments
That you disgrace
Entwining religion and government
When we are a nation
That knew to keep them separate

Especially when a dishonorable man like you
Nearly polluted our debates
With your incendiary preaching
And savaging of justice
Forcing people out of their houses
To vote against your blasphemous candidacy
Soiling the soul of their state
Known for its lynching and racism
Its KKK Pettus bridge
Crossed by civil rights marchers
Bloodied by police
During those halcyon olden days
That will not be perpetuated
By your further political rise
As decency has vanquished
Your personification of *menace*
Threatening a future
We can now tentatively celebrate
With hope for better months ahead

Cartoon by Gary Oliver

Jeff Sessions

Donald Trump's Attorney General

Jeff Sessions – USA Attorney General
April 23 2017

Jeff Beauregard Sessions III

Former Senator from the racist

State of Alabama

Has angered mokes from Hawaii

To the brave policemen of Manhattan

He declaims that a judge

On an island in the Pacific

Can block the President

Of our sacred union

From instituting a muslim ban

Consistent with his own lifelong racism

Framing non-white individuals

As second-class citizens

He now the Attorney General of the USA

Blatantly spreading his outdated agenda

Stating gang murder after gang murder

Is on the rise

    a serious epidemic

Because of illegal immigrants

In New York City

Where its degraded cops

Are "soft on crime"

When if he had checked the data

He would have known

That what he outrageously affirms

Is at an all-time low

DeBlasio the Mayor

Immediately demanded a retraction

While the police commissioner

Expressed his initial "blood began to boil" reaction

Upon reading the words of Sessions' incitement

Donald Trump

Richard Nixon USA President #37

Resigned 1974 due to Watergate scandal

CLAUDE MAYERS

Trump And Nixon

Collusion on the bridge

Deep Throat in the garage

At two in the morning

Espionage and subterfuge

Make for intrigue

                      tomorrow

There always the urge

To preserve the status quo

Even if it is slipping

Into insanity

Power corrupts the vulnerable demented

Brilliant or focused

On goals that mean so much to me

Wounding justice

Crippling freedom

Spying on the citizenry

Paranoid and vindictive

Certain in their victory

Trump and Nixon

Surmounted the rule of law

Behaving like they were immune kings

When they were actually temporary stewards

Of the nation's presidential office

Not to be confused

With dictators

Or authoritarians politicizing the police

And our intelligence community

Wait A Few Weeks Before You're Impeached
(I've Got To Get The Book Out)

Don't decompensate before my eye

Wait a few weeks

Before you're impeached

Tell more spontaneous lies

As you smile for the public

Feeling sick inside

All the chaos you create

Starting to grind your mind

To mush and distraction

Saying 'Rocket-Man' in a speech

That is supposed to be about taxes

You seeming like an avatar

Of bravado and wealth

Expressing supreme defiance

As the dominoes

        fall down

        at your feet

The sycophants looking for a next place to eat

You supplying their potatoes and meat

Until your guilt

Is finally laid out completely

By the prosecutor you want to defeat

Fire

Destroy

Smear like fat on a pig

You not under investigation

You proclaim repeatedly

You changing your tune

Unable to remember the beat

The locksmith coming

To clean the house

Where you never finish tweeting

About viral journalists

Concentrating on the truth you demean

Indictments arriving

Closer to your doorstep

Voices leaking concern

About your angry paranoia

And

this

could

happen

sometime

in

the

karmic

future . . .

Yes, there is a professional Siberian Basketball League that attracts foreigners, including black American players . . .

Exiled To Siberia

Well, it finally happened
Exiled to Siberia
Where the basketball players
Kneel in the snow
Will Putin FIRE them
As I shouted when I was righteous in Alabama
My followers cheering
They still love me!
Maybe they'll come here
And we'll have another rally
And they'll be chanting about the wall
Despite what Steve Bannon says or does
I followed my gut
        my instincts are always good
That's how I became President
I won that election in '16 by a landslide
I even won the popular vote
Whose final tally Crooked Hillary's people claimed
Had nothing to do

CLAUDE MAYERS

Siberia

Petropavlovsk, Kamchatskiy

With illegal immigrants casting those fraudulent ballots
Committing treason
Oh wait
That's what they claim I have done
Colluding with the Russians
While they hacked into our cyber networks
And my fawning weak kneed Republicans
Not doing anything about my tweeting and ignoring
What was important
Bashing those Arab Gold Star parents
General Kelly knows Obama never called him
About his own son
After he made the ultimate sacrifice
I the greatest patriot
Waving the flag
Demanding black football players stand for the anthem
While their people are dying
Discrimination running wild
The white supremacists coming out of the wallpaper
Like Ted Nugent and Kid Rock
Firing their automatic weapons
Wiping out those inferiors
Who don't belong in our country
That has exiled me

To this land of ice and Dostoyevski
Just because I financed my businesses
With laundered money from Putin's oligarchs
And the Iranian guards
Obstructed justice
Firing the head of the FBI who was investigating me
Loyalty essential
As I have shown Vladimir
Who has welcomed me
To live here in luxury
Behind my fantastic insulated plateglass windows
View of the North Pole
Like Napoleon
When the French tried to isolate him
And his power over the people
Basking in the glory of military victories
Watching the eruption of Pompeii
Akin to me
Threatening nuclear war
With my heart of dynamite

'They shot that old lady…Whose home is the home of the brave by the Statue of Bigotry.'

    – – Lou Reed from the 'New York' CD song: 'Hold On' – 'something's happening here…'

Black NFL Player

I am concerned
For my family
    my wife
    my children
If their car is stopped
If the policeman is prejudiced
If he draws his gun
And threatens or degrades
Or kills someone
Black or brown
We know what it is
To fear authority
Be treated unfairly
        unequally
In what is supposed to be
Modern America

Protesting the war in Vietnam
Or civil rights
Was highly unpopular

With the established masters
Those with white privilege
Who didn't have to care
About discriminatory treatment
Being thrown in jail
Perhaps beaten
While killing cops
Walk free with impunity

Entertain me say the fans
But shut up
    refrain from expressing your angst
We allow you on the plantation
But not to live a normal life

Statement from Patriots Chairman & CEO Robert Kraft:
I am deeply disappointed by the tone of the comments made by the President on Friday. I am proud to be associated with so many players who make such tremendous contributions in positively impacting our communities. Their efforts, both on and off the field, help bring people together and make our community stronger. There is no greater unifier in this country than sports, and unfortunately, nothing more divisive than politics. I think our political leaders could learn a lot from the lessons of teamwork and the importance of working together toward a common goal. Our players are intelligent, thoughtful and care deeply about our community and I support their right to peacefully affect social change and raise awareness in a manner that they feel is most impactful."

LeBron James

CLAUDE MAYERS

N-Word On LeBron's Gate

Racism seethes across America

Under the covers

Graffitied on the gate

Of LeBron James' L.A. house

The day before the NBA finals are to start

White Americans not understanding

What it's like to be a black man

In the USA every day

No matter how high you ascend

On the totem pole of success

You are still vulnerable to the hate

Subconsciously bubbling

Throughout the soul of our country

Whether it slits the throats

Of passengers in Oregon suddenly

Or demeans the hair of black girls

In scattered cities and towns

It continues to continue

Despite laws

And the administration of a Negro President

Whose legacy is being stripped

Of its accomplishments

By an authoritarian ringmaster

Pompous

With his accomplices

LeBron's chance to celebrate his art

His dedication

Summarily brought down

By another brash expression

Of the n-word

Painted onto the entrance

To his sanctuary

That he now has to

Diplomatically explain to his kids

In our nation

Of ever present prejudice

And

Lastly

We must ask . . .

Why Ignore Russian Cyber-Infiltration Of Our Nation (USA)?

Why were the heads of Russia's

Three main spy organizations

Secretly visiting the USA

Was it about counterterrorism

Or sanctions

That Putin furiously wanted removed

That Trump then decided not to continue

Though over 90 percent of Americans favor them

After Russia hacked our elections

Persists in botting and trolling our nation

With cyberwarfare

Why did the Kremlin

Have to tell us of the meeting

One week after it happened

Rather than our own government

Which then released a hyped-up memo

Breaching classified information

Potentially damaging decades

Of intelligence building

Despite formal warnings

Against such 'extraordinarily reckless' action

By the FBI and Department of Justice

The suppressed transcripts

Of GPS-Fusion director Glenn Simpson

Finally reached the public

In which Simpson revealed

That Russia was systematically infiltrating

Conservative organizations 'religious and otherwise'

Including the NRA*

Which gave 30 million dollars to

The Trump campaign

In mid 2016

'Earlier than usual'

While it only gave 10 million dollars

To the 2012 Romney campaign

We know Daddy Donald

Wrote the letter

Falsely stating the Trump Tower meeting

With Russians, including his son, Jared Kushner,

And Paul Manafort in June 2016

Was about 'adoptions'

When it was actually about sanctions

Where are this administration

And Republicans

Leading our country

To be lackeys and losers

Surrendered to Putin's Russia

And its assault on the Western World

Trump never says a negative word

About Vladimir

Is he compromised by his past history

Of money laundering and other serious

Criminal acts

That could lead to his own indictment

Sergey Naryshkin

Head of Russia's SVR = CIA of USA – Late January 2018 secretly visited our CIA with heads of GRU and FSB (respectively, military intelligence organization primarily responsible for hacking our elections, performing cyberwarfare on USA and other nations; FSB is main successor to Russian KGB > Russia's Federal Security Service), a meeting that Russia reported to world one week later. Naryshkin had been sanctioned for his part in Ukraine invasion when he was head of Russia's Duma, and had still been banned from entering USA in winter 2018...

Possibly including punishment for treason

Donald didn't expect
To win the election
He complained about his campaign team
Being "the worst"
Melania cried when the electoral vote tally
Showed her husband had defeated Hillary
Her shedded tears not those of happiness

Now we have to worry
That our future
Could be much too Russian
For boundless patriotism
Will we unmask our prejudiced eyes
To see that we are being betrayed
By our own government
That Vladimir gloats
Behind his vast array of computers
Strategically conquering our people
With lies and cyber attacks

While Donald Trump and his willing confederates

Dismantle our crucial institutions

To Putin's amusement

Only to save

Donald's guilty derriere?

*National Rifle Association = NRA

http://www.businessinsider.com/sergei-naryshkin-bortnikov-korobov-visit-us-sanctions-russia-2018-1

http://time.com/5126082/russian-spy-donald-trump-intelligence/

https://www.reuters.com/article/us-russia-usa-intelligence/russian-spy-chief-met-u-s-officials-in-u-s-last-week-sources-idUSKBN1FJ2PF

https://forum.bodybuilding.com/showthread.php?t=175341291&pagenumber=1

http://thehill.com/policy/national-security/371858-cia-head-defends-meeting-with-russian-spy-chief

https://www.npr.org/sections/thetwo-way/2018/01/31/582059134/russian-spy-chief-reportedly-met-with-u-s-intelligence-officials-despite-sanctio

Thank You to Bernadette Calice for inspiring me in the right direction, to get this book created; William Hoard for your expertise and creativity; and all my friends and fans who have helped me successfully complete the journey to publishing this collection of poems and its embellishments.

Attributions Of Images

Donald Trump [Before 2 American Flags] (cropped, cover and before 1st poem)
Author: Gage Skidmore
Source: flickr
License: Attribute-ShareAlike 4.0 International (CC BY 4.0)
Link to License: https://creativecommons.org/licenses/by-sa/4.0/

Donald Trump [pointing, cropped, on spine of book; taken Oct. 29, 2016]
Author: Gage Skidmore
Source: flickr
License: Attribute-ShareAlike 4.0 International (CC BY 4.0)
Link to License: https://creativecommons.org/licenses/by-sa/4.0/

Screenshot of Steve Schmidt on MSNBC-TV

Playing Dominoes in Domino Park in Little Havana, Miami, Florida
Author: Giuseppe Milo
Source: flickr
License: Attribute 4.0 International (CC BY 4.0)
Link To License: https://creativecommons.org/licenses/by/4.0/

General Valery Gerasimov [cropped]
Author: Joint Chiefs of Staff
Code for pic: 170-307-D-PB383-017
Source: flickr
License: Attribution 4.0 International (CC BY 4.0)
Link to License: https://creativecommons.org/licenses/by/4.0/

Vladimir Putin
Author: Global Panorama
Source: Flickr
License: Attribution ShareAlike 4.0 International (CC BY-SA 4.0)

Link to License: https://creativecommons.org/licenses/by-sa/4.0/

James Comey Join Us
Author: Richard Girard
Source: flickr
License: Attribution-ShareAlike 4.0 International (CC BY-SA 4.0)
Link to License: https://creativecommons.org/licenses/by-sa/4.0/

CDC – taken August 23, 2016
Author: Raed Mansour
Source: flickr
License: Attribution 4.0 International (CC BY 4.0)
Link to License: https://creativecommons.org/licenses/by/4.0/

Roy Moore RmooreRape7
Author: FolsomNatural
Source: flickr
License Attribution 4.0 International (CC BY 4.0)
Link to License: https://creativecommons.org/licenses/by/4.0/

Donald Trump – palms turned up and inward; taken 2/24/17 [accompanies 'Trump And Nixon' poem; and is present on back cover; cropped]
Author: Gage Skidmore
Source: flickr
License: Attribute-ShareAlike 4.0 International (CC BY-SA 4.0)
Link to License: https://creativecommons.org/licenses/by-sa/4.0/

American Nixon [accompanies 'Trump And Nixon' poem; and is present on back cover; cropped]
Author: AK Rockefeller
Source: Flickr
License: Attribution 4.0 International (CC BY 4.0)
Link to License: https://creativecommons.org/licenses/by/4.0/

LeBron James – taken 11/18/09 (cropped)
Author: Keith Allison
Source: flickr
License: Attribution-ShareAlike 4.0 International
Link to License: https://creativecommons.org/licenses/by-sa/4.0/

Head of Russia Delegation Sergey Naryshkin At OSCE PA Autumn Mtg.
Ulaanbaatar, 16 September 2015
Author: OSCE Parliamentary Assembly
Source: Flickr
License: Attribute-ShareAlike 4.0 International (CC BY 4.0)
Link to License: https://creativecommons.org/licenses/by-sa/4.0/

2 Cartoons by Gary Oliver

All other photos Public Domain

All above annotated images included in this book are unmodified, except as noted

Back cover ocean photo into sand by Claude Mayers

"BELIEVE ME" - TRUMP POEMS

www.ingramcontent.com/pod-product-compliance
Lightning Source LLC
Chambersburg PA
CBHW040209020526
44112CB00039B/2841